Digital Photography for Beginners

The Ultimate Guide to your Mastery

Disclaimer:

The materials in this book are to be carried out on one's self risk and neither the author nor the publisher will have any responsibilities towards the consequences.

Table of Contents

Chapter 1
Introduction

Most of us remember the days when all cameras required film. You had no idea what your photos would look like until you dropped off the roll of film at the store and waited a few days to pick them up. Sometimes, you were very happy with them. Other times, your film was under developed or over developed.

It was often a shot in the dark so to speak about what you would get. Thankfully, technology has provided us with the convenience of digital cameras. They use a memory card to store plenty of pictures on the camera. You can see what they look like as soon as you take them. No waiting around and no more film!

A digital camera can be a tool that you use for a variety of events. You may be capturing family gatherings or simple times with your kids. You may be taking shots of the outdoors that you enjoy so much or that new car that is yours in the driveway!

Many digital cameras today are classified as point and shoot. As the name implies, they are easy enough to use. You just point at your subject and click to take the picture. Yet that is going to give you mediocre images at best.

There is a reason that digital cameras offer several settings. They allow you to pick the one that is the best fit for the lighting, the elements, and how close up or far away you want the image of that subject to be.

Too often, consumers assume that if they don't get excellent photos, they need to buy a more expensive camera. Yet what they need to do is spend some time learning how to get the most out of the digital camera that they own.

Take the time to go through the owner's manual with the camera you have. If you've lost the manual, look it up online. Read through the various settings offered so that you can learn how to get better pictures. You can also learn various tips and tricks from this e-book that will help you develop a solid foundation for taking pictures.

Have fun with taking pictures, and practice often. Don't wait until you have a special event to try to take pictures. If you aren't familiar with your surroundings for an event, try to arrive early. By doing so, you can take some practice shots.

Since your digital camera is going to show you the results of those images immediately, you can adjust your settings and try again if you aren't happy with what they look like. Investing a few minutes to set it up before an event starts reduces the risk of you deleting the majority of your photos.

Perhaps you really don't have much experience to work with. You just know you enjoy taking pictures. Maybe you aren't thrilled with the outcome when you view them, but there are methods that you can use to change all of it. That is what you are going to explore as you read this e-book.

It isn't possible to change everything overnight, so don't feel overwhelmed. Just take an inventory of what is going to help you on a personal level. If you have lots of photography experience, maybe you just need to tweak a few things. You may have some bad habits that need to be eliminated.

Make a plan of what you are going to try, and focus on one or two things at a time. Once you see the difference that they make for your images, continue with them. Over time, they will become habit, and you won't have to think about them all the time when you take pictures.

As you start to feel more comfortable with certain changes you make for your photos, you can make a few more. Give yourself plenty of time to learn and to explore the options. No one is going to become an expert overnight so don't be too hard on yourself.

With a positive attitude, a desire to learn, and putting in time to practice, you will do very well. Avoid getting into the habit of only taking pictures when you want them from a given event. That puts a great deal of pressure on you to create the best possible images. Instead, take pictures all the time so that you can improve and gain confidence. Then you will be ready when those events take place!

Many consumers are intimidated when it comes to photography. They believe that you have to become an expert to really do it justice. They don't feel they have the time to invest in learning. Yet what you will find is that it doesn't take you tons of time to implement what you read here.

No matter what your level of experience is at this point in time with digital pictures, now you will have the details you need to make improvements. You will also be able to widen your horizons so that your images don't all look the same in terms of how they are set up.

Chapter 2
Technology behind
Digital Photos

Take a few minutes to search the internet for pictures of older cameras. You will be amazed at how far they have come! Depending on your age, you may only know of digital cameras. If you are a bit older, then you may remember when they needed film for them.

Features to Keep in Mind

The technology that is offered with digital cameras is very exciting. It has changed the way we take photos! Understanding some of the features that are offered will help you to enhance the quality of the images you create with your digital camera.

Sensors

Before digital cameras, film used to be loaded into the camera and that is what the image would be imprinted on. Digital cameras don't use film, and sensors are used in their place. The lens of the camera is able to project the image onto a sensor. Then it is electronically going to store that image on the memory of the digital camera. This is accomplished through the use of pixels. After the shutter closes, the charge from the pixels is going to be converted in order to store the image.

Auto Focus

No matter which brand or model of digital camera you own, there is an auto focus feature. This allows you to have some direction with the camera when you don't know which setting to use. It is also a great default when you are in a hurry to get your camera out and take a shot. You may not have time to pick a setting before that moment is forever lost.

The auto focus feature will automatically find the subject for the image and adjust the focus so that it is the best it can be. The amount of light coming through the lens at that point in time plays a role in that setting.

Image Stabilization

You don't want a great shot to be ruined due to the camera shaking or their being blurred elements in the photo due to movement of the subject. Long focal points can also increase the risk of blurred images. Image stabilization can be enabled on most digital cameras. This will help to increase the chances of a clear and crisp image every single time.

Image stabilization is often referred to in digital camera settings as IS or ISO. This is the technology that has enabled digital cameras to be smaller but to offer higher image quality. Some digital cameras have Intelligent IS which means it will automatically select the right setting for the conditions.

Facial Recognition

Many of the digital cameras out there have a facial recognition feature that is built in. First, this allows the focal point to be easier to manage if it is indeed a person's face. Some of these cameras can even identify different types of settings to use based on the skin tone and the lighting of the person that will be in the image. This can reduce the need for editing later.

Scene Recognition

There are also digital cameras that offer scene recognition. This allows the settings to be automated based on the type of scene. The camera is able to determine if it is a motion scene for example versus one where the subjects will be still.

DSLR

A type of digital camera that you may wish to consider is classified as DSLR. This stands for Digital Single Lens Reflex. If you are serious about photography and have plans for advanced features and abilities, this is the type you should invest in.

DSLR cameras are larger than most point and shoot digital cameras on the market. The point and shoot models are compact. However, this doesn't mean you have a heavy or bulky camera to work with if you go for one of the DSLR models.

One of the benefits with DSLR is that you are able to use a variety of different lenses. They can also be manually adjusted. This ensures that you can get the precise shots that you want.

Chapter 3
Selecting a Digital Camera

As you start looking around for a digital camera, you will be amazed with the many brands and models on the market today. Don't be in a rush to buy one, take your time to get something that is a great fit for your needs and your budget. It is a misconception that you need a high dollar digital camera to take great photos.

Here are some of the things that you want to look at when it comes to selecting a digital camera. As you narrow down your choices based on those that meet your criteria, make a list. Then you can look at reviews online about them. By seeing what other consumers have to say about a particular brand and model, you can narrow down your final selection.

Zoom

The zoom feature is one that can really transform the images you take into something spectacular. The zoom can range from as little as 3× to those that have a

40x. This is the ability to zoom in on the subject for the photos. If you often go to sporting events or concerts, you will find that a high zoom option can help you to capture the images that you want.

Settings and Features

Take a closer look at the other settings and features too that are offered with the digital camera. Perhaps you have kids that play sports so you definitely want a sports/movement setting. This will enable you to take great pictures even when they are moving on the basketball court or serving that volleyball at the net.

Some digital cameras have just a few basic settings and features. These can be great cameras to start out with. If you take lots of photos though and you take them in diverse conditions, you may find more value with one that offers additional settings and features that you can use.

Many digital cameras out there also feature the option to create a short video. This may be something you are very interested in. Make sure the video capacity is clear and that the audio for that brand and model of digital camera is crisp.

Size

You will find that many digital cameras are quite compact. They can conveniently fit into the pocket of your shirt or your jeans. Others are quite a big larger, but still not too large when you compare them to early Polaroid and other brands of film cameras.

Think about what will be the most convenient for you when it comes to carrying your digital camera around with you. Mine is very small, and it fits very well into my purse without taking up too much space. It is also light weight and I like that value too.

Ease of Use

It doesn't matter how great a digital camera is in terms of the quality of the photos if you struggle to be able to use it successfully. Make sure you by one that is easy to use. If you are new to digital photography, don't start out with an advanced camera that you will quickly become frustrated with.

Take the time to read the owner's manual before you start using your digital camera too. You will find plenty of great information about how to use the settings. Such details can help you to get the most out of the camera.

Price

Most people have to adhere to a budget when it comes to buying a digital camera. The price is something that you do want to take into consideration. You don't need the most expensive product out there to take delightful photos. However, don't expect to be able to do much with one that you pay next to nothing for either.

Thanks to the competition in the realm of digital cameras, you will find some very competitive prices. You will also find times when they are on sale and you can stretch the budget you have for such a device.

Also, look closely at the various models of a given brand. There may be a few upgrades in features from one model to the next. If you won't use those features, don't pay the additional cost to get the upgraded model.

Warranty

A warranty is a nice touch when you buy a digital camera. Try to find one that offers you as least 1 year. This helps to show that the company stands behind what they are offering. Take the time to read what that warranty includes though as some of them aren't the best once you review them.

Add-Ons

Do you think that you will be looking to upgrade your digital camera in the future? If so, you may wish to buy one that has various add-ons you can buy. Then you don't have to buy a brand new camera. You just buy other items that allow you to continue to use it in new ways.

Chapter 4
Understanding
Composition

Composition is a huge part of taking quality photos. You want to capture the person, object, or landscaping in a manner that is the most flattering. You want to think about the background and any distractions that may be in that image. Don't worry if it isn't perfect, you can use editing tools too. We will cover that in a later chapter.

There are some basic rules with composition that you need to understand. They can serve as a strong foundation for your photo taking opportunities. The more you practice them, the more they will become second nature to you. Before you know it, you will be able to take some magnificent photos spur of the moment. You won't have to think about composition – it will come naturally.

Identify your Subject

What is it about the image you are about to capture that really gets your attention? Is it the person walking down the street that you are trying to capture or the old buildings around the neighborhood where they are walking? Find your focal point so that you can try to de-clutter the image as much as possible.

Your focal point should be the center of the camera viewpoint. Most digital cameras feature a T or a box that you want to center around that focal point. By doing so in the view box of your camera, you will be able to correctly capture your subject.

If you want a simple way to cut out distractions around your subject, use the zoo feature. It will zoom in on that focal point, and there will be less room in the frame for the elements you don't want.

Don't get into the habit though of always putting your subject in the middle of the image. Try some where the focal point is to the left or to the right. It will really transform your images so that you aren't getting bored with what you see in the formatting from one image to the next.

Background

Do your very best to capture a delightful background around your subject. You can use the zoom feature to help you avoid items you don't want in there too. If you have a great background, back off the zoom to help capture more of it. As mentioned, there are editing tools that we will cover in a future chapter.

That is important to point out so that you don't avoid taking a wonderful shot due to a poor background. Don't delete images off of your digital camera that you love due to something in the background not being right. Those are elements you can learn to manipulate.

Vertical and Horizontal Shots

Most of us get into the habit of capturing images horizontally with our digital camera. After all, that is the way it is designed to be held in our hands. However, you are missing out on some great shots with a vertical display.

This is a wonderful tip for how to use composition that you don't want to overlook. Not sure if an image will look better vertically or horizontally? You don't have to decide when you are taking the photos. Take several in each direction with your digital camera. You can make the decision later on when you review them.

Many people find that taking images of tall buildings, the sky, mountains, etc. seem to look much better if they are vertical rather than horizontal. By simply turning your camera that new direction, it will open up some new possibilities for you!

Moving Concept

You can add the concept that a car or a person is moving too when you take a still photo. For example, maybe you are capturing the image of a brand new sports car coming down the road. It could be images of marathon runners. By taking a photo with the zoom backed off, you get them as the focal point.

Leave enough space in front of the frame though that it looks like they are moving forward. Practice taking this type of shot so that when the moment is right, you can do it without a second thought. This type of composition adds a thrilling dimension to such images.

Personal Preference

When it comes to composition, you have plenty of room for personal preference too. After you understand the technical aspects of all of it, you can decide what you like the best and what you find to be too boring. Just do your best not to get into a routine with every single shot.

For example, don't put your subject in the center of every shot you take. Try the various composition techniques so you can explore them as you take your shots. Then you will have a wide variety of types of images that you can be proud of.

Foreground

Just about everyone that uses a digital camera is familiar with background. It can make or break a given image for you. What is often overlooked though is the foreground. If you shoot at a wide angle, you will be including quite a bit of foreground in your shots.

Try to include interesting objects, colors, and textures that will help you to really make your image stand apart from the norm. You want the photo to be created in a way that draws the viewer's eyes to the focal point.

Zoom

Avoid getting into the habit of taking images with the subject too far away. Use the zoom feature that is offered on the camera to help you get a closer view, without having to move closer to the object.

Chapter 5
Use the Lighting to your Advantage

Light is an important part of taking quality pictures; even if you are taking those images at night, even if you are taking those images in a dark area such as at a concert. In fact, the word photography is Greek and it means light writing. Too much light and you have bright spots in your pictures. Not enough light, and you have dark shadows.

The ability to use the lighting to your advantage is going to transform the quality of your photos. It doesn't matter what the subject happens to be. It doesn't matter if they are indoor or outdoor images. Don't be nervous about playing around with lighting either. You can create a certain mood or element in your images with something as simple as a change to the lighting offered.

Back Lighting

When the source of the light comes from behind your subject, it is referred to as back lighting. You need to make sure you use it to your benefit though so that it won't case dark shadows that you don't like in your photos. When you use it as a way to create a silhouette though, then it can make a regular picture something that has exceptional artistic elements.

There are a couple of things to take into consideration when it comes to your digital camera and the use of back lighting. There is a metering mode on your digital camera, and it is responsible for the lighting conditions. Think of it as the brain of your camera. It determines the best shutter speed to use to create an image.

However, what the automated settings on the camera determine to be a great image to create doesn't always align with what your own brain thinks. You can manipulate the setting in order to make back lighting work for you to create something very unique and original.

One way to get the changes that are going to work for you is to use the matrix metering setting. This is going to help your account for all of the differences in lighting that will affect your shutter speed for the image to be captured.

If you have a background that is bright, your dimly lit subject in the photo is going to become under exposed. This is what results in a silhouette. If you don't want that, you need to use the fill flash setting. This is going to fill in the required amount of light around your subject.

Side Lighting

Side lighting is an element that many people don't understand. It can hinder the value of the images you capture with your digital camera. It has to do with the angle of the light source. As a result, part of your subject is in the light and part of it has shadows.

When used correctly, side lighting can add a dramatic element to your photographs. A great way to do this is to get a person to pose in front of a window. They should stand in a manner that allows one shoulder to be facing the camera.

In order to really capture what you are after, take several images. Have the subject slowly move in the different images so that you get more of their body turning towards the camera than when you first started.

What you will notice when you go through those images is that they are different due to the intensity of the lighting and the amount of shadow that covers their facial features.

If you find that side lighting is occurring in your photos, but you don't want it, there are a couple of things you can do. First, you can use the fill flash as mentioned above. This will fill in the shadows with more lighting so that you can get a brighter subject in the images you capture.

Another option to experiment with is to use natural lighting. Turn off the flash so that you get a softer effect in your photos. If you are inside, you can use poster board or other white surface to reflect the light off of.

Diffused Lighting

A type of modified lighting source to consider using is called diffused lighting. It is a wonderful tool that will reduce the risk of your photos being over exposed or filled with lighting that is rough for the eyes to look at.

With diffused lighting, your goal is to soften the lighting so that it won't be so harsh. Depending on where you are taking a picture, the natural elements may be harsh. You don't want to miss a great photo opportunity because of it.

The best conditions for outdoor photos are on a day when it is cloudy and overcast. Then you have lighting, but it isn't too harsh. You can create that same type of effect with your digital camera with the use of diffused lighting elements. Try to avoid taking photos during the time of day when the sun is brightly shining right above you.

Doing so is going to offer too much light, and it will wash out the colors. It will also result in shadows in your images that are very dark. Try to use natural lighting when you can so that you can turn off your flash. This will offer a softer effect to the images than using auto flash.

Artificial Lighting

The opposite issue of too much lighting is not enough of it. When that is the case, you can count on artificial lighting to help you get the results you seek for your photos. When you use the built in flash for your digital camera, which will be a form of artificial lighting. The problem with this is that it increases the chances of red eye for the subjects in your pictures.

An external flash is one option to consider, but you must have a digital camera that has some advanced features. If you do end up with red eye, don't delete your pictures! This is a very easy fix with editing software tools.

Additional Lighting Tips

The right lighting plays a vital role in the quality of the images you take. Try taking pictures in each of these types of lighting situations. Practice one and make sure you understand the best settings for your digital camera before you move on to the next.

Here are some additional lighting tips that you want to keep in mind:

• White balance needs to be adjusted any time you are using indoor lighting
• Only use built in flash when necessary, try to rely on natural sources of light
• Zoom in for subjects that are at a distance to manipulate the lighting

Chapter 6
Common Mistakes to Avoid

In addition to learning the fundamentals for better digital camera shots, you need to know what to avoid. If you have been taking photos for quite some time, you may have developed some bad habits. They may be tasks you are comfortable with, but you will need to make an effort to change them if you want better looking photos.

If you are new to taking photos, then you do want to learn about these common mistakes. They are pitfalls that you want to avoid. By being aware of these types of common mistakes, you can create better photos from the start!

Change Position

Most of us take photos from a standing position. There are times when you are at events when you will be seating. They are comfortable positions, but if you change your location, you change the outcome of the images.

For example, when you are photographing children, get down on their level. Sit on your knees so that you get their bright faces and not just the top of their head and then a downward angle in the photos.

If you have limited mobility, it is going to be fine for you to take your shots in the manner that works for you. Don't risk hurting yours body or being in a position that is painful in order to change your photos up.

Turn Flash on and Off

Don't get into the habit of allowing the auto flash to always be on with your digital photos. Turn it on and off manually depending on the type of composition that you are after. If the lighting isn't flattering with it on, turn it off. Rely on natural lighting for your photos any time it is available.

Black and White Images

Some digital cameras offer a black and white setting. This can add a rustic appearance to your images. If you don't have such a setting on your camera, don't go buy a new one. Many of the software programs for editing offer this feature. You can use it to quickly change any color photo into a black and white.

Get your Camera Out

Try to have your camera with you just about anywhere you go. Get it out and use it rather than leaving it at home or in the car. Take pictures from all angles and in all lighting conditions. Take many photos too, even if you delete all but a handful of them each time.

Have fun using your digital camera, and don't stress so much about the outcome of the images. Don't be overly critical about them either. If you don't have the shot just perfect, use editing tools and software to make them better. You will improve if you incorporate what you learn here and you avoid common mistakes.

Experiment with the Settings

You aren't going to mess anything up with your digital camera if you change the settings. Don't be afraid to work with them and see what they offer. Try the various models and features that it offers. Read your owner's manual to discover what they do.

Try taking the same image with several different settings. Do this one after another so that you can see firsthand the differences that occur with such settings. This is a great way to practice with your camera. Then when you are taking action shots that can't be replicated, you will always feel confident you have picked the right mode and settings.

Reset your Settings

A common mistake though is not remembering to reset your settings. Try to get into the habit of resetting before you put your digital camera away. That will prevent you from picking it up to take a shot in a hurry and realizing the setting is wrong. You would fare better if they are on default settings when you are in a rush.

The default for ISO is going to at least offer you something basic and good enough for most of the subjects you wish to capture. If you have some favorite settings, you can reset to those before you put the camera away.

Memory Card

The last thing you want is to start taking photos and then to discover your memory card is full. When you get a new memory card, make sure you format it. Delete old photos once you have uploaded them to your computer. Otherwise, you may be in a rush to delete them when you want to take new shots.

Holding your Camera

Since most digital cameras are small and light, many people get into the habit of holding them with only one hand. While you can take shots like this, it isn't the most stable. A one handed shot can result in blurred elements or shaky looking images.

Get into the habit of holding your digital camera correctly. It needs to be held still when the shutter button is pressed for the best outcome. Even a small amount of movement can make a difference.

Your dominant hand should be on the top part of the camera. Allow your forefinger to hoover closer to the shutter. That way you can press it when you are ready to take your shots. For stability, your thumb should be on the back part of the camera.

Use your other hand to cup underneath the camera. You can also put it around the lens if you find that to be more comfortable. Some digital cameras have grips in place so that your hands feel very comfortable in those locations.

You can offer your body extra stability too by leaning on a tree or a vehicle if you are standing up. If you take the photos sitting down, try to prop your elbow of the dominant hand up on the arm rest of the chair. If you are kneeling, you will need to learn to balance on your knees so that you aren't rocking during the shots being taken.

Chapter 7
Tips for Improving your Shooting

Don't just point and click with your digital camera. Think about what you really want to capture in each shot. Slow down and you will realize that you are getting much more than you realized. This gives you a moment to adjust the focus of the subject, to look at the foreground, and to evaluate the background.

By doing so, you will find that you delete far fewer photos than before. You will be able to use the tips and tools that you learned about in this e-book to take images that really capture what you would like for them to. You have the ability to do this; you don't have to be a professional photographer!

Steady

Hold camera as stead as you can, from start to finish, for each shot. If you are moving, then your images are going to be blurry or fuzzy. If you find that it is very hard for you to remain steady, invest in a tripod. This will hold the camera in place for you.

Reduce the Zoom

Another reason that you may end up with blurry or fuzzy images is that you have the zoom all the way to the highest power. Reduce it some and you will find that it significantly improves the appearance of your images.

Comparisons

Try two different techniques when you have free time to take pictures. Then you can compare the outcomes of them based on the techniques that were used. You may find that you like certain features for a given subject but not others. Comparisons will help you to determine quickly which settings to use to get the outcome you want when you take photos.

Read

There is a wealth of information out there that will help you with better photos. Such information pertains to the specific brand and model of digital camera that you use. There is an owner's manual that comes with it that will explain to you how to set up everything for different types of pictures.

If you don't have that original owner's manual, you should be able to find it online. Look at the diagrams too so that you can identify the locations for the different settings in the menu.

When it comes to troubleshooting, ask questions. You can do so on the website for that brand of camera. You can join online forums for free where you can share information and ask questions from other members.

Frame Tight

Next time that you are watching a movie, pay attention to the close-ups. You are able to look into the eyes of the subjects. You don't see the tops of their heads very often in such shots. You don't want to leave much room above the head, and you can even completely take it off.

I know this is hard to adjust to as we have often been told not to cut off the top of anyone's head in a photo! That is true with a distance photo where you get their entire body. With a close up, you want the focus to be on the facial features, especially the eyes or a smile.

Natural versus Posing

Take some posed photos now and then, but most of the time you want them to be natural. This is especially true if your subject happens to be animals or children. Allow them to do what they normally would, and you can just be on their level to snap plenty of great digital photos as they do so.

The Rule of Thirds

It doesn't matter if you are new to photography or you have been doing it for quite some time. The rule of thirds can help you to be able to take better quality photos. You can use this rule as a way to enhance your creativity, not hinder it. Painters use this rule too, and it is dated back to the early artists of Greek images.

The name is actually misleading though, and you will understand more why in a moment. In fact, many that have dealt with the rule of thirds will tell you that it should have been called the rule of ninths. The concept involves taking a rectangular shape. Then it is divided into 9 smaller rectangles, all equal in size.

For the best results, you want to place your subject focal point where the inner lines intersect:

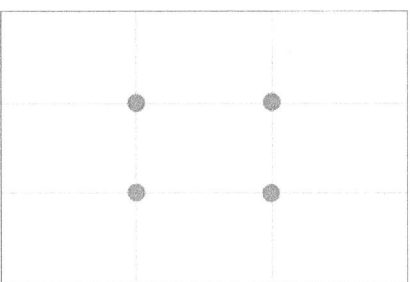

By doing so, you add more balance overall to the photos. It will be very pleasing when you or someone else looks at it. The eyes will naturally gravitate to the focal point you had in mind instead of some random element found within a given photo.

Walk yourself through it

If you walk yourself through the shots, you will find that they come out much better. First, ask yourself what is the story that you want the photo to tell others? What will their impression be about what is taking place in that photo? You are essentially trying to capture the emotion of any given moment with any given subject.

What is the focal point of the image that I want people to see? With a quality digital picture, their eyes will immediately go to that focal point. If it doesn't, then you need to modify the type of shot you are taking. At the same time, ask yourself if there are any other focal points in that frame that could compete with what you wish to share.

For example, you may be trying to capture the awe of beauty of a flower garden. Make sure that is what you capture in the image. If you capture another focal point in the image, then others may be looking at it instead.

Ask yourself if there are any distractions in the background or the foreground. You can use the zoom to help you with eliminating background elements you don't want to have in place. You can also edit them later on with software tools.

I have seen great photos of a couple, and it is distracted by clothing in a pile in the background. Maybe there are plates and a pizza box sitting on the table beside them. Such distractions take away from the beauty of a picture so be aware of them as you take your pictures.

Does my subject fill the frame? If you don't feel that it does, you need to zoom in. Otherwise, your focal point can be lost quickly in everything that is surrounding it in the image.

If you aren't sure about how you should take the shot, try it more than one way. What is really thrilling about a digital camera is that you can often capture several photos in a very short period of time. You can try one horizontal and then one diagonal of the same subject.

You can try one with the zoom out and then one with the zoom closer in of the same subject. Don't be afraid to take tons and tons of shots. Then you can keep those that best capture the story that you want the picture to tell.

Chapter 8
Additional Equipment to Consider

As your love of photography grows, you may find that you need some additional items to keep going with it. Most of them are inexpensive, and they can help you to keep your digital camera safe when not in use. Others allow you to make sure you keep it fully charged.

Case

Get a hard case for your digital camera that is waterproof. It only takes dropping it once without a case to cause damage. When your camera isn't in use, have it in the case. Then if you drop it, the camera won't get marked up, the screen won't get scratched or broken, and you can go about your business.

A good case will cost you less than $20. It is one of the first items you should buy when you get a digital camera. While it is optional, it isn't a good idea to go without one. Try to find a case that holds your camera snuggly. If there is too much room, it can be damaged from jostling around all the time.

Extra Battery

There are plenty of unhappy people out there that go to take photos, and realize their battery is dead. They may get a few shots, and then that is all. Always have an extra battery for your digital camera. Keep it in your hard case so that you can quickly access it and insert it into the camera. This will save the day!

Car Charger

It is a good idea to keep a car charger in your vehicle for times when you can't charge the batteries at home. Just plug one end of it into your camera. The other goes into the port in your vehicle. Within a few hours, you will have a fully charged battery.

Filters

Your digital camera may allow you to add filters. These are disks made of glass that screw onto the lens. They can completely change the appearance of your digital pictures. There are filters that allow you to add some warmth to your images. They are perfect for shots taken mid-day when there isn't enough natural lighting to do them justice.

If you find that your images are too reddish or orange, you can add filters that will cool them down. They add more blue tones to the scene. Neutral density filters can help with removing fast moving elements from scenes. Other filters will reduce the glare from a shiny surface in your image. This is known as polarizing.

Tripod

If you want to be able to take your tripod with you easily, get one that folds up. Then you can place it into a camera bag. You can take it out and set it up in a matter of seconds. A tripod offers you more stability than if you are holding the digital camera.

Basics

Start out with just the basics and then you can build from there. Once you decide the direction you will take with your photos, it is easier to justify the additional accessories and equipment.

Compatibility

Before you purchase any accessories to use with your digital camera, make sure they are compatible. Many of the products out there are universal, but that isn't always the case. You need to ensure that they will work for your type of digital camera as well as the brand. If you aren't sure, contact the manufacturer of that accessory and ask.

Bundles

You may be able to save a great deal of money on your accessories if you buy them as a bundle. This is buying a group of items instead of each one individually. Just make sure the cost is going to offer you value. The bundle should cost less than buying each included item separately.

You also want to make sure each item in the bundle is something you will actually use with your digital camera. If the answer is no, don't buy a bundle as the value won't be there. You will be spending money on items you just don't need.

Used Items

If you really want some accessories but the cost is holding you back, consider buying used items. You may be able to find them online, at garage sales, or even at your local pawn shops. Ask for verification that these items work though before you pay for them. You don't want to be out the funds by learning that they don't once you get them home.

Chapter 9
Finding Inspiration

If you enjoy photography, finding your inspiration isn't going to be difficult. What often holds people back though; is that they don't like the quality of the images. That can be frustrating and it can cause them to stop taking photos.

The fact that you are gaining valuable insight throughout this e-book though means that doesn't have to be the outcome for you. Instead, the materials here can give you a clean slate to work from. If you are new to photography, it can give you the encouragement you need to get started.

If you have some experience, the materials can help you to fine tune what you already have in place. It can help you to problem solve too so that some of the mistakes you have experienced will be part of the past. Finally, you will be able to find inspiration from the fact that you are delighted with the way your images come out.

Trust your Instincts

While there are some tried and tested rules of orography, you should also trust your instincts. Don't get so wrapped up in those rules that you fail to allow your creative side to be part of the images. Trust yourself to make good choices too about the settings to select and how you use the environment around you.

No, you won't always be impressed with those choices. However, that is part of the overall learning experience. Photography is very hands on, so by trying it out, you learn what works and you learn what doesn't.

Try New Things

With that being said, don't be afraid to try some new things. Don't take your photos the same way every time. Change the lighting, change the focal point, and change the types of images. Instead of always sitting or standing, try kneeling or try using a tripod. When you try new things, you continue to be inspired when it comes to your photo taking.

Kids

If you want to have fun with taking photos, kids are a wonderful way to be inspired. First, kids don't seem to mind their pictures taken as much as adults. They aren't self-conscious about hair and weight, so you can just snap those shots. Kids also have an innocence to them that really makes photos come to life.

If you have your own kids, take pictures of them all the time. You will be happy you did later on too because they grow up in the blink of an eye. If you don't have your own kids, ask a friend or neighbor if you can take images of their kids so that you can practice your photography skills.

Animals

If you have any pets, take pictures of them. You can take action shots as well as those why are still. Many animal lovers find plenty of inspiration in such photographs. You can also go to the zoo or your local animal shelter and take lots of pictures of various animals.

Nature

Sadly, most of us have such a fast paced lifestyle that we fail to see the beauty that nature offers us. Take pictures of the beach or the mountains where you live or where you visit. Take pictures of the trees as they change with the various seasons. No matter what time of year it is, nature has something magical to offer if we open our eyes to it.

Weather Patterns

Many people enjoy taking photos of the changing weather patterns. They find inspiration in doing so. This can be the swirling of clouds as a rain storm is coming through. It may be the rainbow that opens up with the sunlight after it rains.

Special Events

Try to take photos at special events that take place around town. This could be an outdoor concert in the park or a parade through town. Take pictures at all events that you attend. You will find that it will provide you with a variety of forms of subjects that you can use to take photos from.

Night Shots

Your digital camera has settings available that help you with taking night shots, practice taking them too. It will enable you to take a wider variety of photos.

Try to take them as the sun is just going down as well as when it is completely gone.

The various moon phases will offer you different amounts of lighting for your night shots. They can provide you with plenty of inspiration as you compare the different phases in your photos.

Make Time

Even though you are busy, make time to take photos. Get into the habit of always having it with you. If you get a compact digital camera, it can fit into your purse or your pocket. Then you don't have one more thing to carry around with you.

Make the time to review your photos soon after you take them. Upload them to your computer so you can see the images. It is going to be fun to share them with other people. You can create online albums and you can even order prints that you would like to have actual copies of.

Continue to Learn

Regardless of your current level of talent, continue to learn. Challenge yourself to understand and to implement the basics of taking quality photos. Select a few middle-of-the-road options and work on them. Then you can pick a few difficult strategies and also practice them.

As you keep on learning, you will find that your passion and your inspiration continue to grow. Don't put photography on a back burner. It can be a great stress reducer too!

Encourage Yourself

Don't get into the habit of just picking up on what isn't right with a given photo. Give yourself credit for being active with photography and for trying new things. Focus on what you did right too. Encourage yourself so that you will want to continue to take pictures.

Chapter 10
Editing Tools

In several areas of this e-book, we have mentioned editing tools. These are tools that allow you to make changes to the photos you have taken. Some of the common edits include:

- Removing red eye
- Changing background colors
- Enhancing overall colors
- Brightening photos
- Darkening photos
- Boarders
- Modifying background
- Cropping
- Changing color to black and white

With editing tools, you can have fun playing around various changes. If you like what you created, save it to your computer. If you don't, start all over. You can use these tools for "what if" elements.

Learning

Editing tools give you a chance to learn new things. It also means that photos you initially thought you may have to delete can now be saved. Even if you have great photos, you may wish to enhance them.

Experimenting

The freedom you have to experiment with editing can help you to relax too with taking photos. You aren't going to be so stressed about trying to get the perfect photo captured each time. Just do your best, and then you can use these tools to make them better.

What you will likely discover is that in the beginning, you are using editing tools for basic things quite often. However, as your picture taking skills improve, you will have those elements in place with your images. Then you can use the more advanced editing features.

Creating

With the help of such editing tools, you can create something very unique and impressive. You can take a basic photo and make it something that you treasure. You can also create photos books or collages that you give to others as gifts.

Software Packages

Take your time to find the right software packages to use. Your computer may already have some of those tools offered for free. Some software packages are very inexpensive and others cost more than you may wish to spend. Make sure you get value in regards to the types of features that are offered.

You also want to read reviews about software packages. This will ensure you get one that is easy to use. It doesn't matter how many editing options it has if they are difficult for you to figure out how to use them.

Chapter 11
Conclusion

Nothing captures memories like photos! Digital cameras have transformed the way we are able to take pictures. We can immediately view them. We can also use software to edit them. We can share them on our computers as well as order hard copies of them.

Beautiful photos don't happen by change though. They are the combination of someone with a passion or inspiration looking for a shot to take. Understanding the basics of taking digital photos as well as some of the options you can consider for lighting and composition increase the chances of delightful photos.

There are plenty of differences out there from one digital camera to the next. It isn't about buying the most expensive model though. It is about learning and about trying new things. You can explore the various settings on your digital camera and then take pictures so you can see how they make a difference.

Understanding the rule of thirds, composition, and lighting really do enhance the quality of the photos you will be able to create. Learning new methods for getting your subject into focus and as the focal point is also important. Using the background and the foreground to your advantage also helps.

We can't always control the setting of a photo. However, we can strive to capture what we really want people to look at when they see that photo. With that in mind, take your time to see everything when you look through that lens.

After you learn the basics and you are familiar with your digital camera, you will have a good idea about the settings to use for different elements and occasions. Of course you also have to take into consideration what you want that outcome to look like.

For example, you may want a close up of the subject or you may be interested in a silhouette of it. Knowing your options and how to make them materialize is going to put a smile on your face!

Enjoy learning the best practices for taking digital photos. You are going to have a great time as you do so. Over time, your images will get better and better. They are going to be a priceless treasure in the future too!

Learn all you can about your particular camera too. That way you can access the menu and make changes when you want them for your images. You can also reset those settings easily without any hassles.

Create a cheat sheet if you need to at first. You can keep it in your camera case as a quick reference. Write down the best settings to use for certain types of shots or certain lighting conditions. Over time, you will memorize those settings and you can toss out those notes.

They can be very useful at first though so you don't become frustrated. You don't want to be out there trying to take pictures but spending your time struggling with settings. You want the time you spend taking photos to be fun and to be a great way to expand your knowledge.

With the great digital cameras out there and so much knowledge to share, professional looking pictures aren't just offered by actual professionals. Don't be surprised when people are complimenting you on those you have taken. They may be interested in learning about what type of digital camera you have too. They don't realize that isn't the only variable.

Any given digital camera can have plenty of options to pick from when it comes to the settings. Learn many of them so that you can use them for your photos. You can rely on the basics as well as some of those advanced settings to set your photos apart from the rest.

Take the time to find the best digital camera for your needs and your budget. The opportunities for taking wonderful photos are all around you. Now you have the opportunity and the knowledge to take your very best shot every single time! Don't leave the outcome for amazing photos to chance or luck!

Bonus Chapter
Understanding
Astrophotography

What is Astrophotography?

There is so much that can be done with your digital camera after dark! The term astrophotography refers to taking pictures of anything not on the Earth. As soon as you point your camera to the sky and take pictures of the stars or the moon, that is what you are taking part in!

You don't need a high tech digital camera or expensive equipment to take such images either. In fact, there is a good chance you already have everything you need on hand. You can decide to upgrade to some better equipment later if you become passionate about astrophotography.

Even though we don't see it in movement, the Earth is turning on its axis throughout the day and the night. This means that there will be movement in such images you capture with a digital camera.

Selecting a Digital Camera for Astrophotography

If you plan to take part in astrophotography, consider a DSLR camera that has removable lenses. This gives you more control and more range when it comes to ISO and shutter speed. They can also be hooked up to your telescope.

Digital snapshot cameras don't have removable lenses and they have exposure times that are limited. They are low cost and they can be used for your daytime digital camera needs too. However, they aren't going to work well for any type of deep sky images or long exposures.

You can also buy a digital camera that is specifically designed for this type of image taking. They are called astronomical CCD cameras. They reduce noise and they have value for both science and imagining. However, they can be very expensive and complex to learn all of the features they offer. You will need a computer to use them too.

What Types of Images do you wish to Capture?

There are several different types of astrophotography that you can take part in. Scenic images are the most common. They include wide angle shots of the moon or the Milky Way. You can use any type of digital camera with short exposure settings of 30 seconds or less. For the best results, use a tripod.

If you would like to take images of planets, including the moon and the sun, you will need a digital camera with high resolution. This is going to help you to capture details such as the craters on the moon or the many details of a given planet.

Deep sky astrophotography involves taking pictures of the various clusters of stars and the galaxies. You will need a low noise digital camera for the best results. You also need one that offers long exposures.

Lighting

In order to keep them in focus and to have enough lighting, you will need to use long exposure times. Some of these exposure times can be as long as two minutes to get a great image. You need to be patient if you would like to turn this into a hobby or something more.

Shutter Speed

In order to gain more lighting as you take photos of the sky and its elements, you need to understand shutter speed. Recording the most light as possible is the underlying element you need in place for exceptional astrophotography. The shutter determines how much light will hit the sensor.

When the shutter is open for an extended period of time, you will capture more light. You can also use a larger hole which is referred to as the aperture in order to capture more light. You will have to keep the shutter button held down on most digital cameras in order to keep the shutter open.

Depending on the digital camera you own, there may be tricks and settings you can use that will allow the shutter speed to be longer than the typical settings. Check your owner's manual and also check around online in forums to get feedback from others about such settings.

Focus

Make sure you understand the settings for your digital camera so that you can get the focus correct.

You need to be able to turn off the auto focus feature. Use the manual focus that is called infinity – this is the farthest that the camera will focus.

If you struggle with focus, rely on crossed dowels that are in the front of the imagine scope. You can use the magnification from the digital camera or you can magnify them when you upload them to your computer.

There are pieces of equipment called a right angle finder that you can use to make focusing easier too. The downside is that they range in price from $150 to $200. It is an investment to consider if you are going to be taking plenty of shots of the stars, planets, and the sky.

White Balance

Find out if your digital camera has a white balance setting, most of them do. Most of them have it turned on as a default setting. You will need to go into the settings and change it. If it is on default, it will reduce the clarity of your night time images.

If there is light pollution, then your images will look shades of red or brown. The Tungsten setting is a great option to consider for long exposures for the sky at night.

If you have a higher end digital camera, it may offer some other customized settings for the white balance. If you can tweak the colors in your settings, do so. Change the blue/amber balance and the magenta/green balance. You will love the improvement in the colors for your night time photos.

ISO

If you are new to taking astrophotography shots, use the ISO 1600 setting. This is for shorter exposures which is what you want to do in the beginning. As your experience broadens and you are ready to take longer shots, you can adjust ISO.

T-Mount Adapter

A T-Mount is a piece that attaches your camera to your telescope. With an adapter, you will be able to take your shots through your telescope. You should use the self-timer on the camera to help you with this. Set it for 30 seconds so that you aren't using your finger to take the shots. That can increase the chances of moving the telescope and creating blurred shots.

Wireless Remote

If you would like to the exposure time to be longer than 30 seconds, use the bulb setting on your camera. Many of them have this setting and it is the next option after the 30 second choice. If you will be buying a digital camera, and want to use it for this type of photography, make sure you have that setting available from it.

The shutter will stay open in this type of scenario as long as you would like for it to be. You will have a wireless remote hooked up to it so that you control that function. Yet you don't touch it so that there is no risk of the telescope moving as you do so.

Some great cameras to consider for this are the Canon models. The Rebel series all offer a simple, mini plug for the bulb release function. Nikon models also offer this with an infrared remote release. For those that rely on the N3 plug in, you will need to purchase a plug in that fits that particular brand of digital camera.

Some set ups also allow you to use your computer as the wireless controller. There is software that you need to set up so that the computer, the camera, and the telescope can all work as a unit.

What Exposure do I Want?

When it comes to astrophotography, determining what exposure you want is very important. Yet it can also be one of the most confusing elements that stand between you and quality shots. The equipment you have and the location for the shot will influence the exposure you want to use.

Since there are so many scenarios, your best option is to test out a shot when you get started. What you will do on a cloudy night is going to be different than what you will do on a clear night. Take a test exposure and then look at the histogram featured on your LCD screen.

The histogram shows you the amount of pixels that an image holds based on the brightness of the shot. To the left, you see the darker pixels and to the right you see the brighter ones. Each camera has instructions for reading the histogram. Make sure you know how to use this data. Then you can adjust your settings and take another test shot. Continue to do this until you have the balance you want.

Star Trails and Galaxies

A tripod is a great tool for your digital camera to help you with astrophotography shots. Star Trails can take from 15 minutes to several hours to capture. Yet the lovely stars that will be found in your images are certainly worth it!

If you would like to take photos of galaxies and other details, you will need to get a telescope. You can attach the digital camera to it so that you can look through the telescope and capture your shots. You will need an equatorial mount in order to secure it in place.

Image Processing Software

Don't worry if you don't get the perfect shot you were hoping for! Practice makes perfect, and the more you take part in astrophotography, the easier it gets. In the meantime, you can use image processing software. This allows you to make adjustments to the digital images you take.

You will be able to brighten them or to adjust the color. You can also change the amount of contrast. There are quite a few of these software programs out there for an affordable cost. It can be fun to play around with the various features.

Take lots and lots of shots when you are outdoors, even if many of them look similar. Transfer all of the images to your computer through your memory card or a USB cable. Look at them all using 100% magnification. Don't worry if they look grainy, that is normal.

Keep the images that you like the most and delete the rest. Now you can work on improving those that you are going to keep. Change the magnification to 25% and you will notice that the grainy appearance is gone.

Give it a Try

Now that you know all of the opportunities out there that occur when you explore astrophotography, give it a try! Use your basic equipment to begin with and see how you like it. You may find that you really enjoy taking these types of images. You won't look at the vast sky again in the same way. You will realize all the beauty that it holds that we often overlook.

If you find that this type of photography is for you, then you can consider some of the upgrades and add-ons. They will allow you to continue to challenge yourself and to try longer shots.

You do need to be patient when it comes to astrophotography because it isn't as quick paced as what you normally experience. However, the payoff is that you get some amazing photos that no one else has. You are going to be blown away by all of the details you have captured.

www.ingramcontent.com/pod-product-compliance
Lightning Source LLC
Chambersburg PA
CBHW072308200526
45168CB00014B/1029